MARVEL
AVENGERS ASSEMBLE

1000 Stickers

01477593

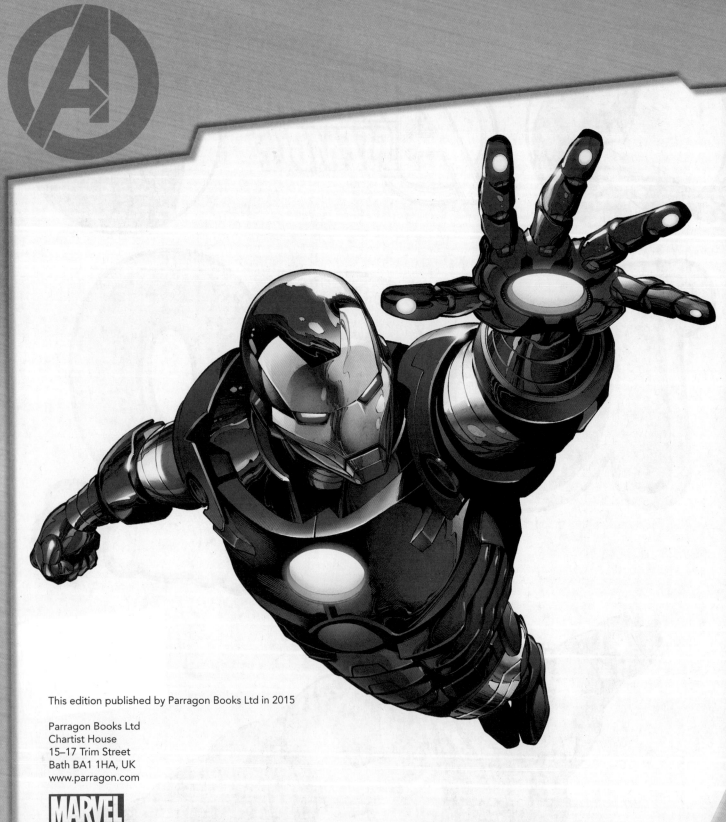

This edition published by Parragon Books Ltd in 2015

Parragon Books Ltd
Chartist House
15–17 Trim Street
Bath BA1 1HA, UK
www.parragon.com

MARVEL

ISBN 978-1-4723-9125-4

Printed in China

1000 stickers

Can you find the following items
hidden throughout this book?

 x1   x2

 x3   x4

PaRragon

Bath • New York • Cologne • Melbourne • Delhi
Hong Kong • Shenzhen • Singapore • Amsterdam

Heroic sticker activities

Use your stickers to complete the mighty puzzles and activities!

The Avengers are assembled and ready for action! Use your stickers to complete this picture to match the one on the opposite page.

Powerful puzzle

Use your stickers to recreate this wall-smashing picture of The Hulk!

Super sequences

Can you work out which mighty hero comes next in each sequence? Use your stickers to complete the rows.

Clue to a Hero

Read the clue then add the correct stickers to reveal the heroes.

A This powerful warrior was cast out of Asgard and sent to live among humans on earth.

?

B This agent is not one of the Avengers … but he gives the orders.

?

C This hero used to study gamma radiation – the source of his superpowers.

?

D This Avenger learned most of his weaponry and acrobatic skills with the circus.

?

E This agent was born and raised in Russia and is an expert spy and martial artist.

?

Answers on page 63

Find the imposter

The Avengers are ready for action, but there's something not quite right about one member of the team.... Find your red cross sticker and put it on the phoney warrior.

Answer on page 63

Warrior colouring
The Chitauri are coming. Colour this vicious villain.

Ready for battle

Hulk and Thor are ready to protect Earth.

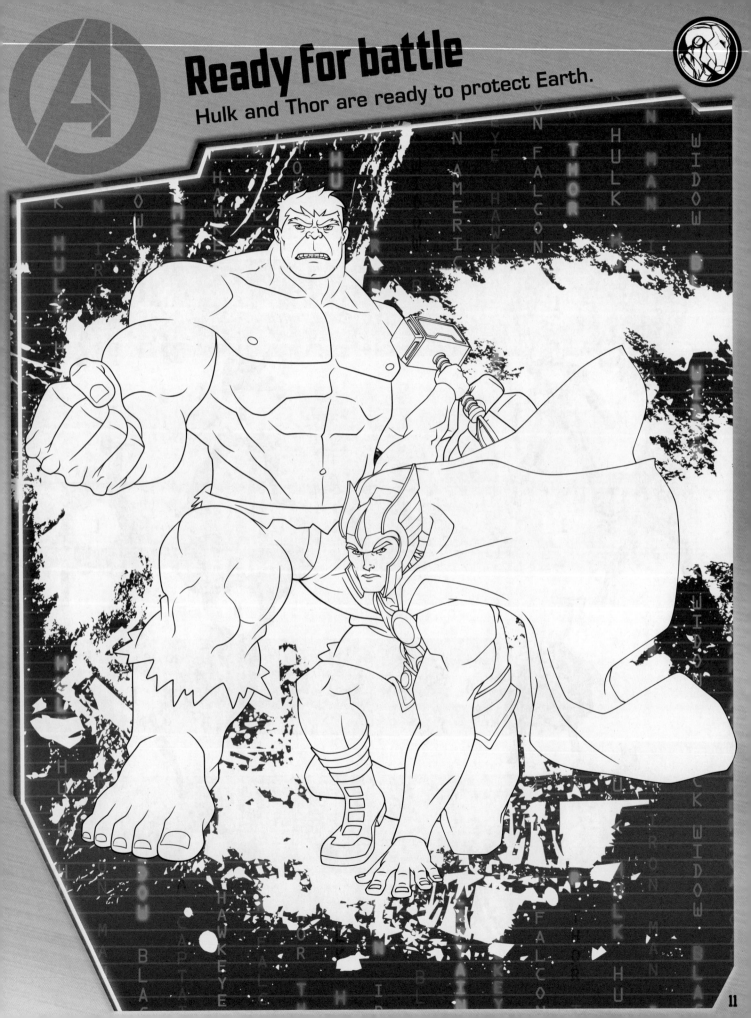

Shadow matching

Draw lines from each shadow to the matching Avenger then place the correct sticker over the shadow.

Answers on page 63

Overheard heroes

Which Avenger would say each of these phrases?
Put the correct sticker below each quote.

1

"You wouldn't like me when I'm angry!"

2

"I never miss."

3

"Bring the thunder!"

4

"Fighting for equality, justice and freedom."

5

"Armour: activate!"

Answers on page 63

Mini missile!
Iron Man fires a missile from his armour.

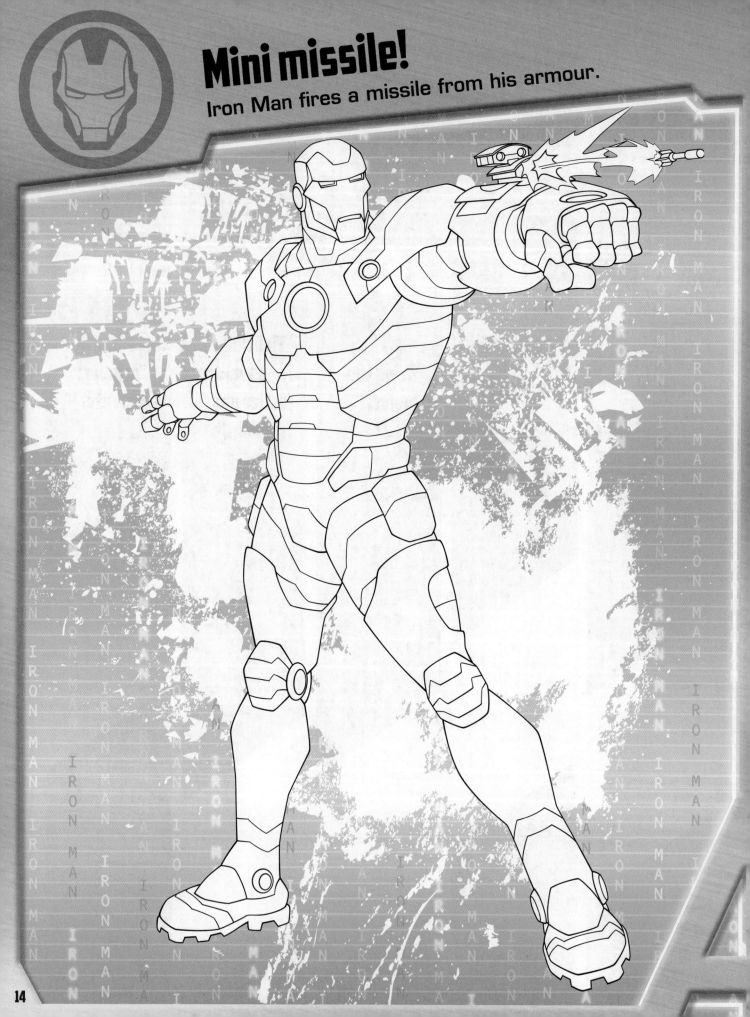

Mighty Thor!

The Prince of Asgard charges into battle.

Three in a row

How to play
Play this game with a friend.
1. Each player chooses a Super Hero or villain.
2. Take it in turns to place your stickers into the grid.
3. The first person to get three in a row wins!

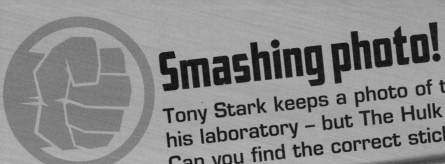

Smashing photo!

Tony Stark keeps a photo of the Avengers in his laboratory – but The Hulk has smashed it! Can you find the correct stickers to complete the picture?

Hulk smash!

The Hulk is amazingly strong.

Crack the whip!

Anton Vanko stole Iron Man's technology – now he fights against him as Whiplash!

I-spy a villain!

Black Widow is an expert spy – right now she's tracking three super villains! Which trail leads her to their leader – the menacing mechanical M.O.D.O.K.? Once you've found the correct path, place your villain stickers over their shadows.

Answers on page 63

Super snapshots

It's hard to get good photographs of Super Heroes and super villains – they move too fast! Can you tell which Avenger, or which villain, appears in each of these blurry photos? Put the correct sticker in the square.

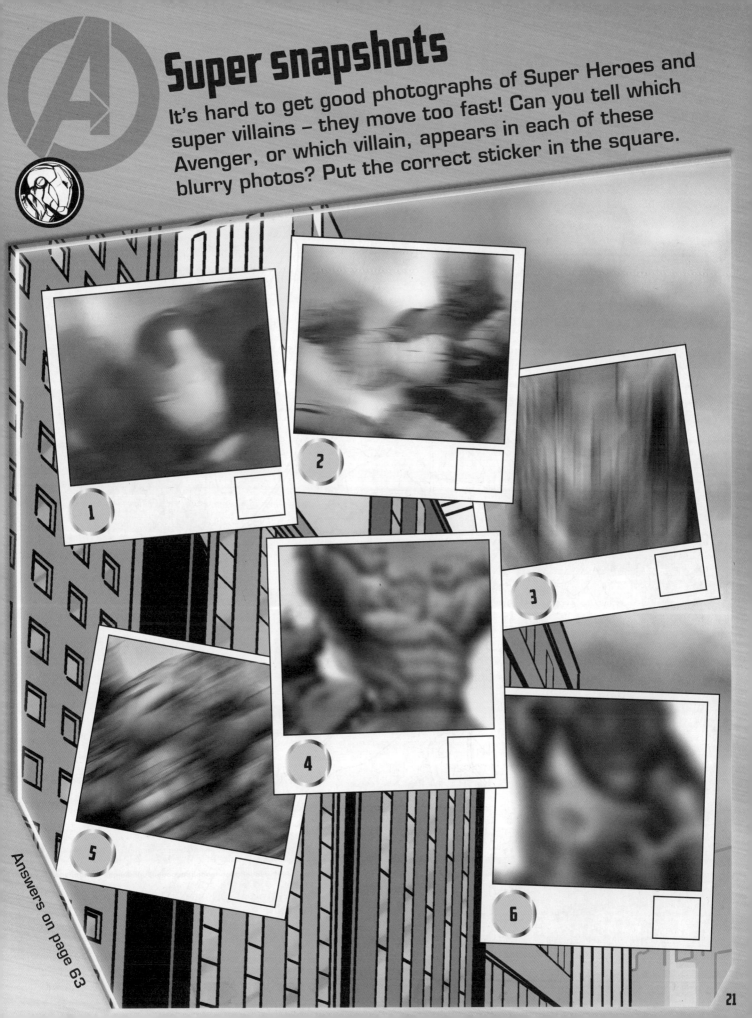

For freedom!

Captain America is a man out of time – but he's still the same Super Soldier!

Defending the Earth

Nick Fury is the current Director of S.H.I.E.L.D.

Mighty differences

There are seven differences between this picture of Earth's Mightiest Warriors and the one on the next page. Place an Avengers logo sticker on the next page every time you spot a difference.

Double trouble!

Hawkeye fires two explosive-tipped arrows at once!

Travel in style

Tony Stark invented the Aven-Jet Prime to transport the Avengers at super speed!

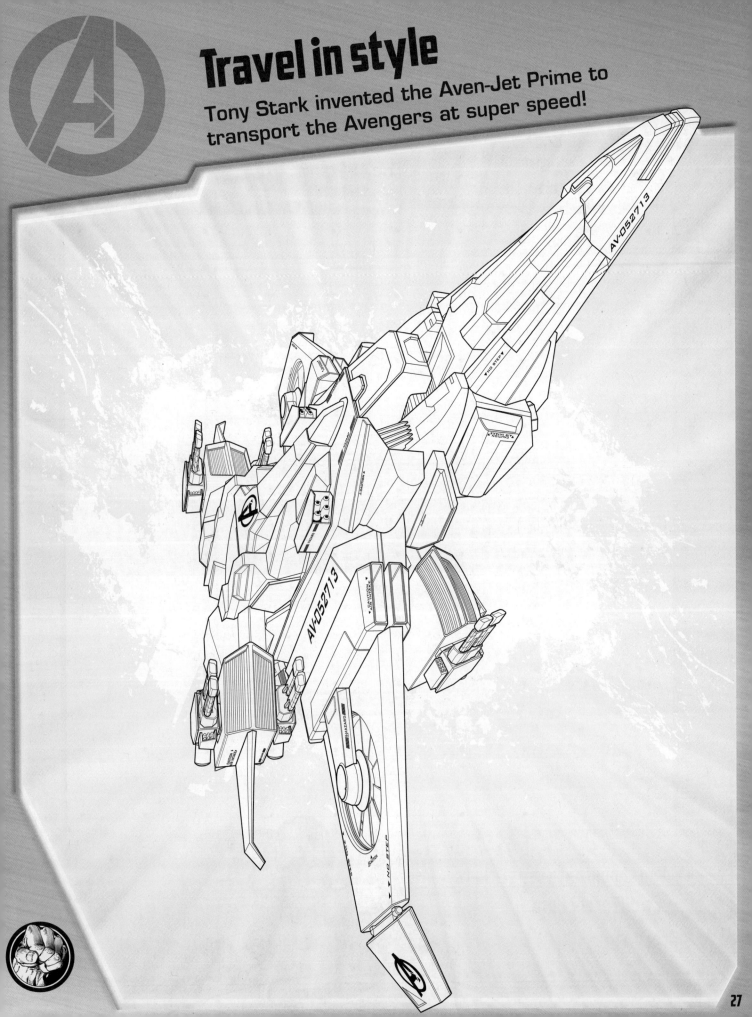

Cap's boxes

Take turns with a friend to draw one line between two dots, horizontally or vertically. If you complete a box on your turn, put a sticker inside it. When the grid is full, the person with the most stickers wins!

You should each use stickers of a different hero.

Make a scene

Use your stickers to recreate this scene on the empty background at the bottom.

Iron Man match-up

Only one of these shadows of the Armoured Avenger matches his true form – place your Iron Man sticker over the correct one.

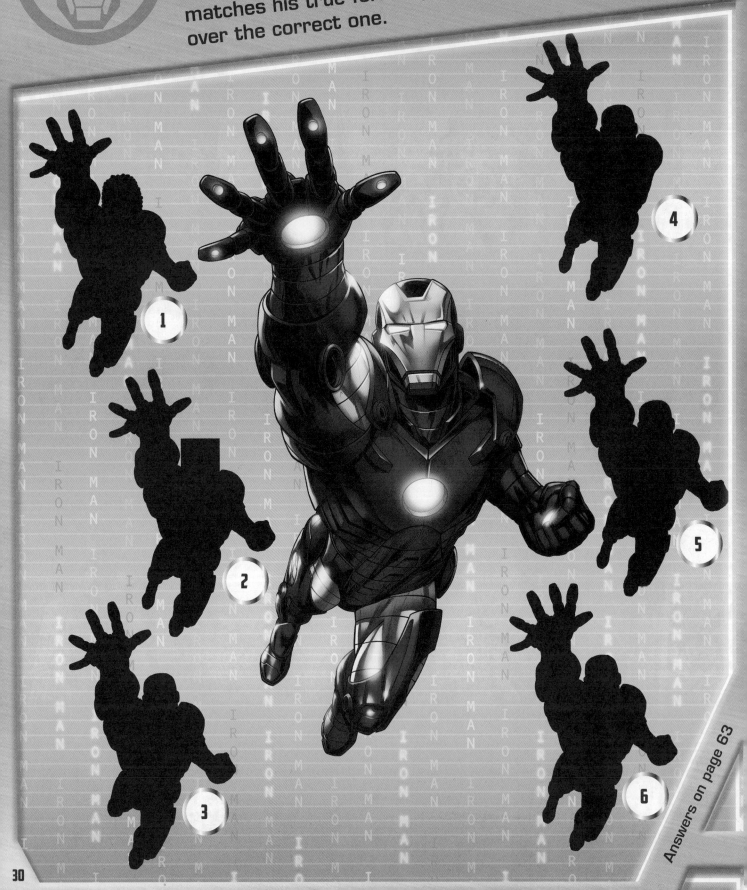

Answers on page 63

Super villains

The Avengers have come together to face the enemies no single hero could withstand. Use your stickers to match each villain to their description.

1 He used to be Johann Schmidt, head of HYDRA, until a failed version of the Super-Soldier Serum turned him into a powerful super villain.

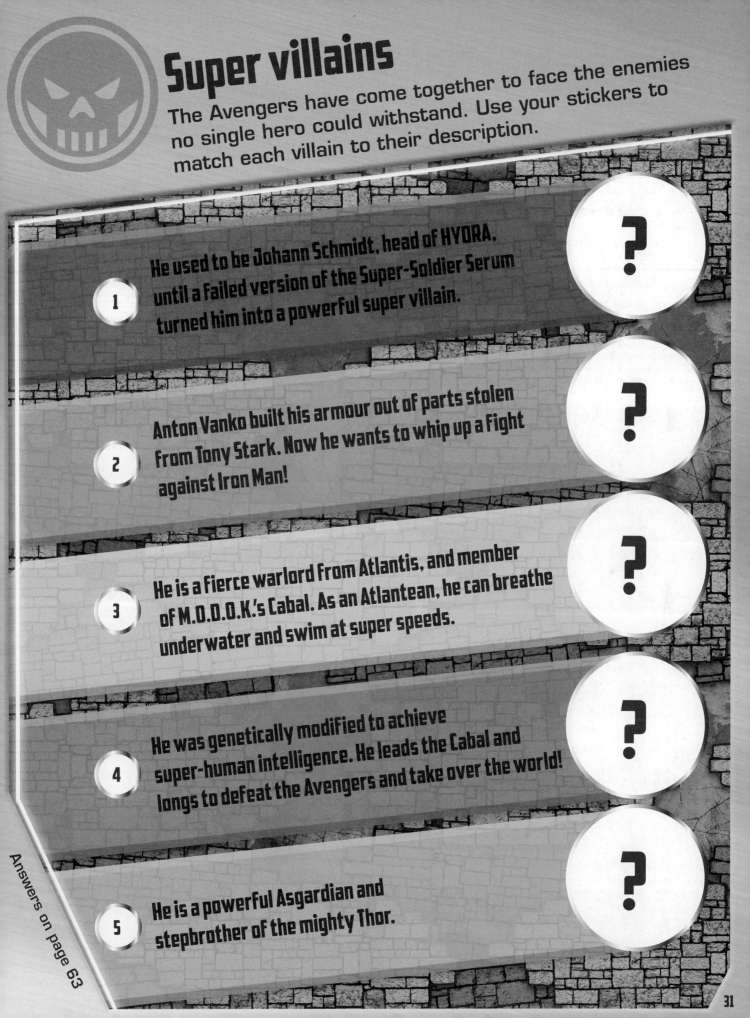

2 Anton Vanko built his armour out of parts stolen from Tony Stark. Now he wants to whip up a fight against Iron Man!

3 He is a fierce warlord from Atlantis, and member of M.O.D.O.K.'s Cabal. As an Atlantean, he can breathe underwater and swim at super speeds.

4 He was genetically modified to achieve super-human intelligence. He leads the Cabal and longs to defeat the Avengers and take over the world!

5 He is a powerful Asgardian and stepbrother of the mighty Thor.

Answers on page 63

Mischief maker

Loki longs to rule Asgard and defeat his brother, Thor.

Wings of fury

Falcon's holographic wings let him fly and fight at the same time!

Winged Avenger

Once Falcon has fired parts of his wings he has to regenerate them. Can you help him by adding the missing 'feathers' to his wings?

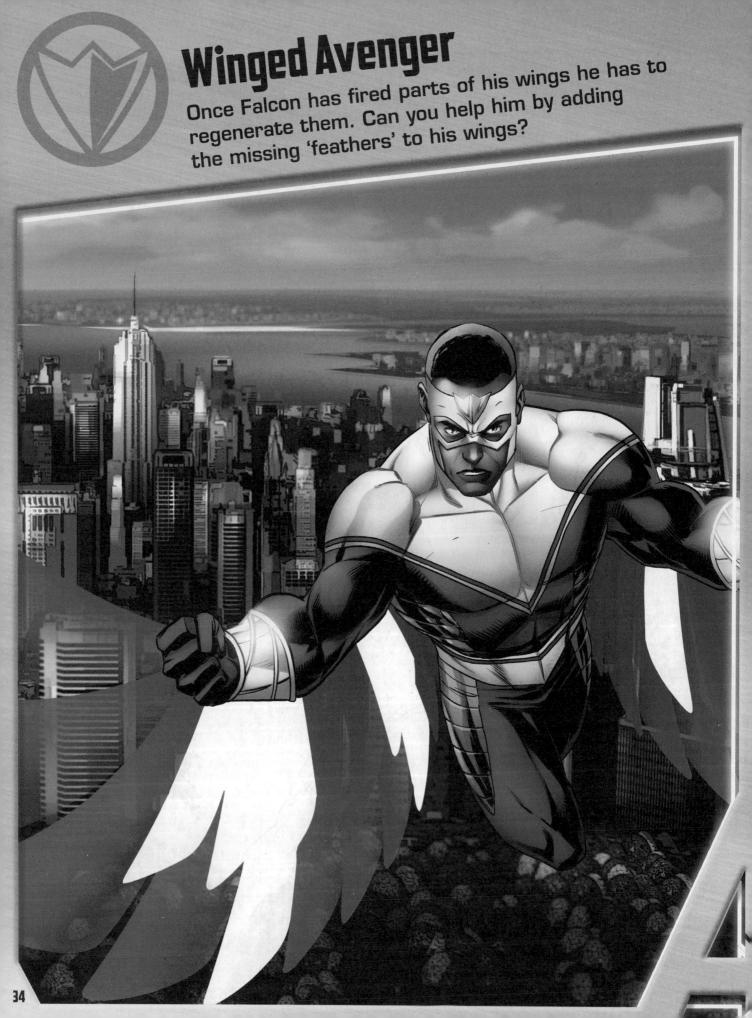

Sharp shooting

Hawkeye's arrows never miss! Look at these targets for 10 seconds, then close your eyes and stick an explosive arrowhead on the villains. Be careful not to hit Captain America, though!

Action-packed activities

Join the Avengers by completing these activities and puzzles.

How many Captain America shields can you find hidden among the Avengers?

Answers on
page 64

Back to base

After a fight with the evil Cabal, the team is heading back to Avengers Tower. Can you help them find their way?

START

FINISH

Answers on page 64

Draw Thor

Copy this picture of the Prince of Asgard into the grid below. Then colour him in before he goes into battle!

Throw-down

The Avengers have cornered the evil Red Skull. Thor throws his mighty hammer, Mjolnir, Captain America hurls his Vibranium shield and Hawkeye fires an Ensnarement arrow. Follow the trails to see which one of them hits HYDRA's most fearsome agent.

Answer on page 64

Warrior changes

There are five differences between these two pictures of the Avengers. Colour in an Avengers logo for each difference you find.

Head of HYDRA

Red Skull will stop at nothing
to conquer the world.

Perfect landing

Iron Man lands with a SMASH!

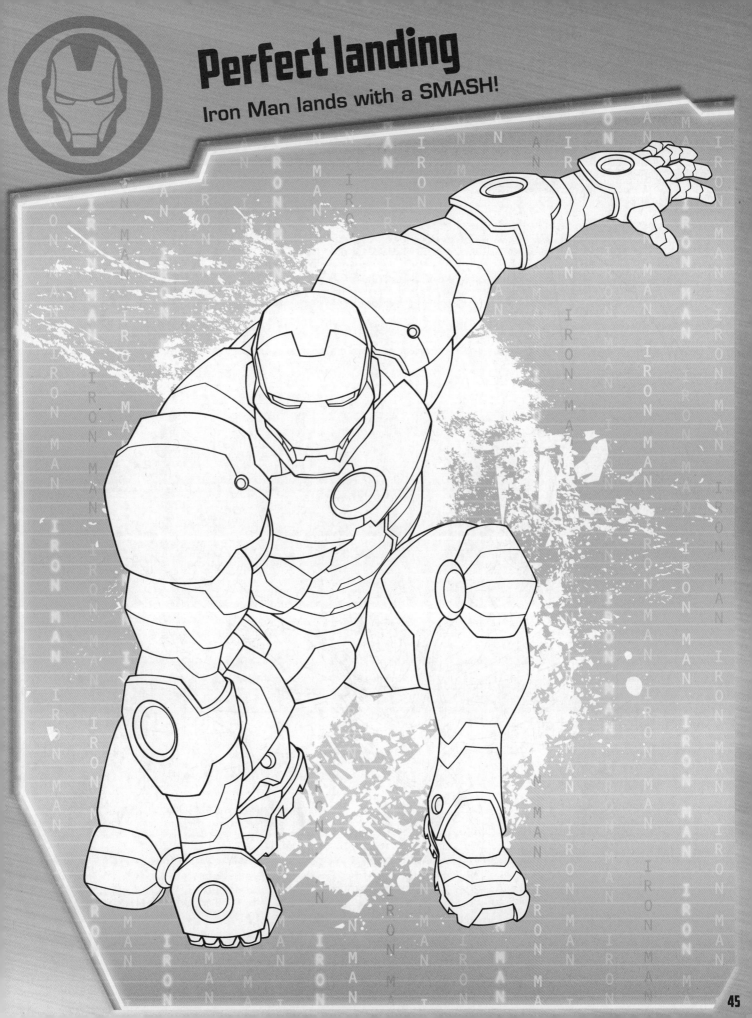

Power failure

Falcon must fly fast to join his Avenger teammates – but he's lost power to one of his wings! Can you join the dots to bring it back online? Then colour him in!

World-saving wordsearch

Test your spying skills by finding these words in the grid. Look forwards, backwards, up, down and diagonally.

S	I	E	S	V	R	E	G	N	E	V	A
U	O	U	R	O	S	L	U	P	E	R	C
P	G	S	M	H	S	U	O	P	R	I	R
E	E	A	S	J	E	L	E	O	S	N	O
R	A	I	M	D	S	G	W	P	D	T	B
S	E	R	U	M	E	T	A	T	T	B	A
O	A	V	E	I	A	H	H	C	E	I	T
N	I	M	S	H	N	U	E	O	W	S	A
I	E	Y	P	S	S	N	E	B	J	O	M
C	S	A	S	O	O	D	L	E	I	H	S
S	B	P	T	S	N	E	K	P	T	S	O
M	J	O	L	N	I	R	S	S	U		

REPULSOR
AVENGER
SHIELD
ARROW
THUNDER

SERUM
GAMMA
MJOLNIR
ACROBAT
SUPERSONIC

Iron Man match!

Only two of these pictures of Iron Man are correct. Can you find and circle the correct two?

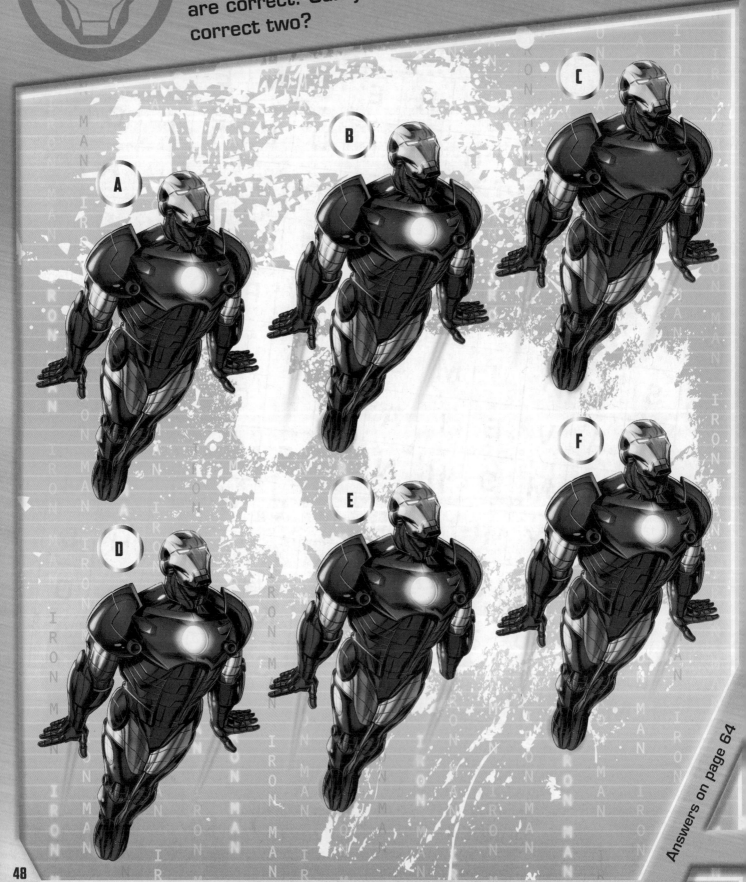

Answers on page 64

Brutal battle armour!

Iron Man and Falcon both have powerful armour that helps them fight the mightiest of foes. Use this page to design your own Super Hero suit!

Will you be able to fly?

What will your weapons be?

Will you have wings? Or rocket boosters? Or soar through the air in a flying vehicle?

What colour armour will you have?

49

Silent spy

Black Widow fights with the Avengers ... but she keeps an eye on them for S.H.I.E.L.D. as well!

Abominable villain

Gamma radiation plus Super-Soldier Serum make for one powerful villain – Abomination!

The fog of war

Hawkeye has fired a gas arrow to confuse his enemies – can you see through the thick gas cloud and work out which evil villains he's up against?

A

B

C

Answers on page 64

52

How many HYDRA?

HYDRA agents are skilful soldiers and utterly loyal to their leader, the Red Skull. How many agents can you count on this page?

Answer on page 64

There are _____ HYDRA agents.

Strong words

Tick the box that completes each Avenger's sentence.

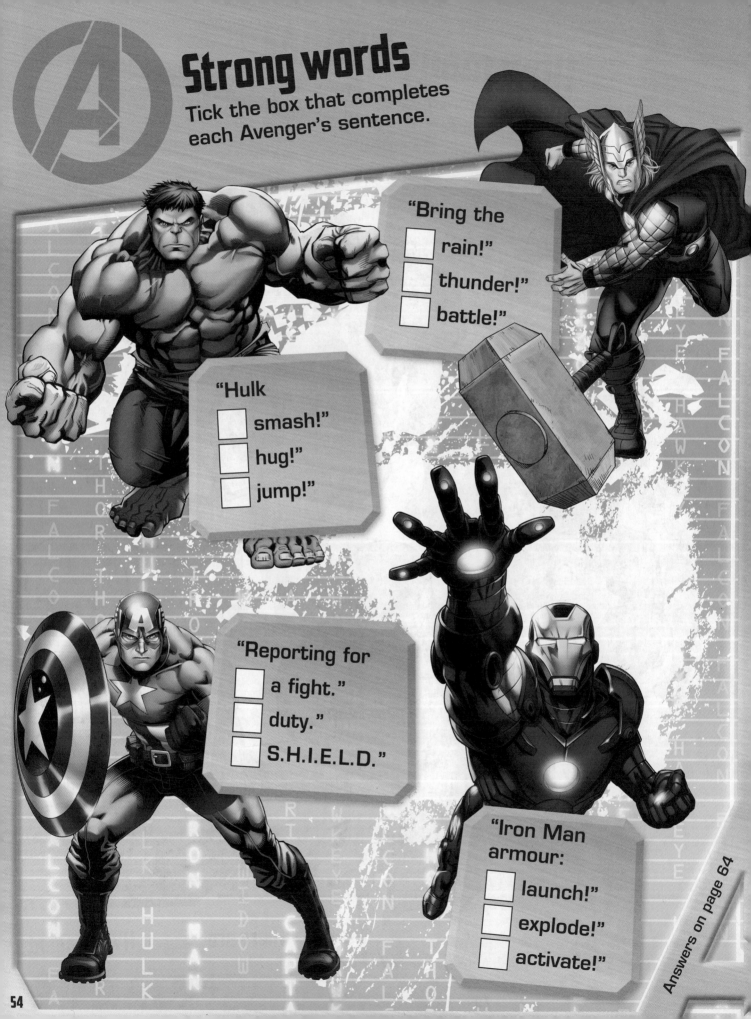

"Bring the

☐ rain!"

☐ thunder!"

☐ battle!"

"Hulk

☐ smash!"

☐ hug!"

☐ jump!"

"Reporting for

☐ a fight."

☐ duty."

☐ S.H.I.E.L.D."

"Iron Man armour:

☐ launch!"

☐ explode!"

☐ activate!"

Answers on page 64

Private training

When you don't want to be disturbed, cut out this door hanger and hang it on your door. Or, if you want some company, turn it over to let everyone know.

Ask an adult to help you cut around the dotted line.

© MARVEL

S T A Y

A W A Y

Warrior training in progress.

Path of courage

Captain America is rushing to take on the alien Chitauri – follow the code that will lead him into battle!

START

FINISH

CODE

UP LEFT RIGHT DOWN

Copy colouring

Look at this picture of the Mighty Thor
and copy the colours on to the page opposite.

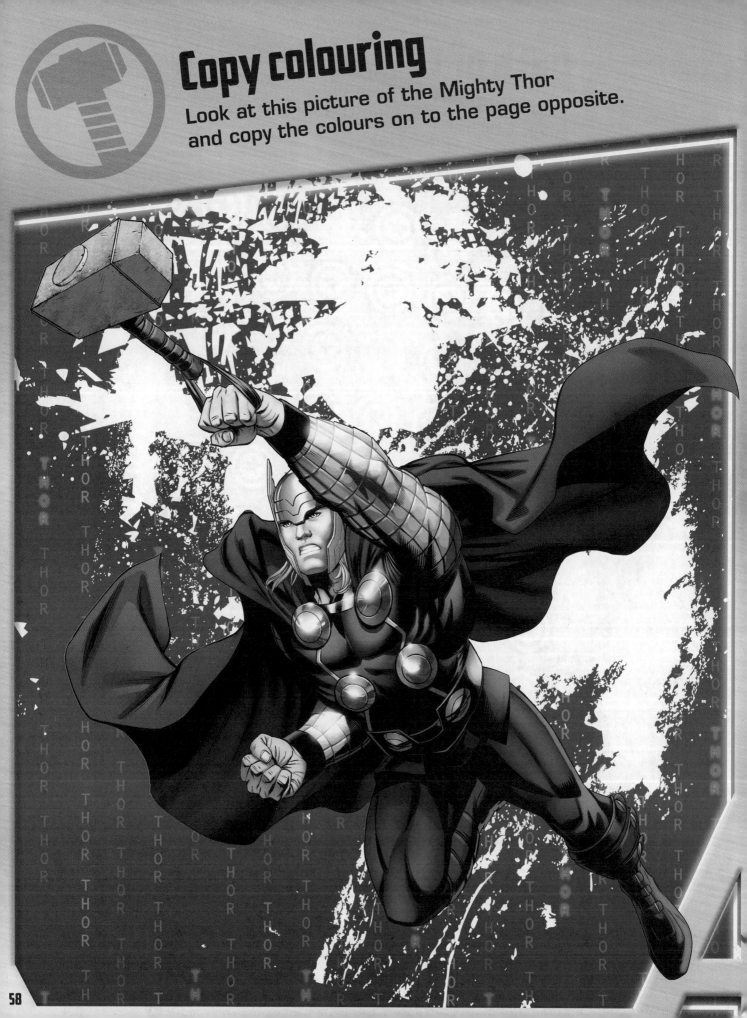

THE MIGHTY THOR

Test your powers

How much do you know about Earth's Mightiest Heroes? Test your knowledge of the Avengers with this quiz.

1 Which Avenger's real name is Clint Barton?

Thor

Iron Man

Hawkeye

2 Which TWO Avengers can fire weapons from their suits?

Iron Man and Black Widow

Iron Man and Hulk

Black Widow and Captain America

3 Where is the Avengers' headquarters?

Stark Tower

Avengers Tower

Avengers Lair

4 What country is Black Widow from?

U.S.A.

France

Russia

5 What colour are Falcon's wings?

Black

Red

Blue

6 What kind of radiation changed Bruce Banner into The Hulk?

Gamma

Alpha

Banna

7 Thor's mighty hammer has a name – what is it?

Asgard

Mjolnir

Attuma

8 Iron Man's real name is _____?

Donald Blake

Nick Fury

Tony Stark

9 Iron Man's armour is red and _____?

Silver

Blue

Gold

10 With which organization do the Avengers work to protect Earth?

S.H.I.E.L.D.

HYDRA

A.I.M.

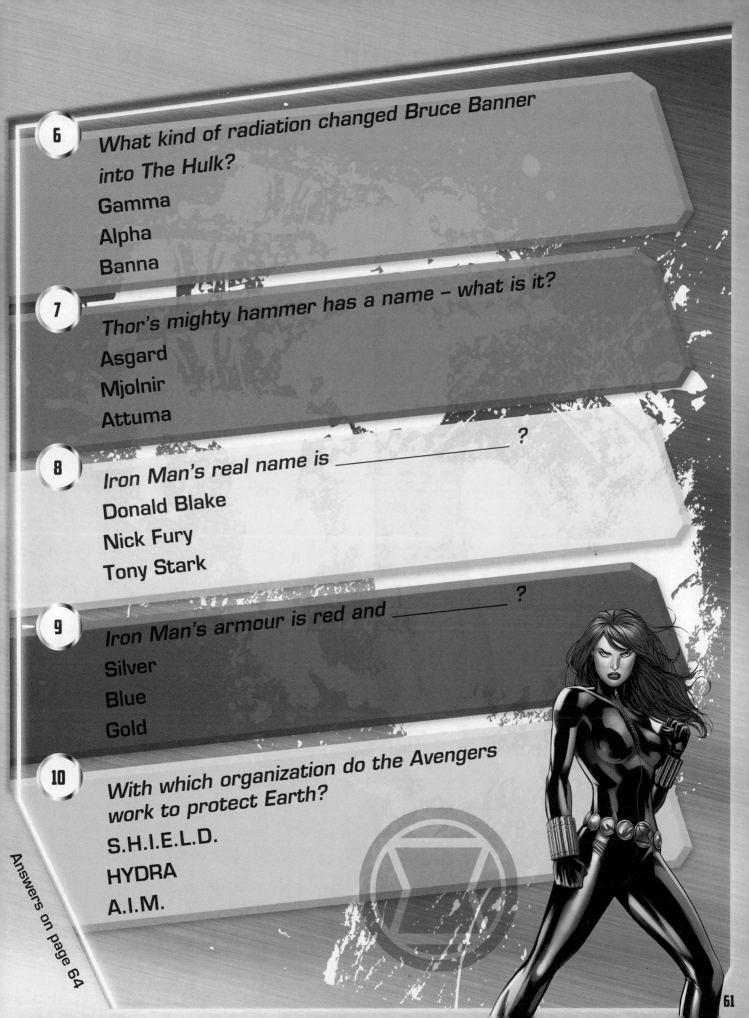

Answers on page 64

Draw The Hulk

Draw the other half of the
Jade Giant, then colour him in.

Answers

Page 7

A   B   C

D   E

Page 8

A   B   C

D   E

Page 9

Page 12

1–D, 2–A, 3–B, 4–C, 5–F, 6–E

Page 13

1. Hulk, 2. Hawkeye, 3. Thor,

4. Captain America, 5. Iron Man

Page 17

Page 20

B

Page 21

1. Iron Man, 2. Nick Fury, 3. Loki,

4. Abomination, 5. Hulk, 6. Red Skull

Page 25

Page 30

5

Page 31

1   2   3

4   5

Did you find all the hidden items?

Page 11 Page 12 ★ Page 9 Page 43 Page 7 Page 27
Page 21 Page 48   Page 55   Page 36

Pages 36-37

There are nine shields.

Page 40

Page 42

Page 43

Page 47

S	I	E	S	V	R	E	G	N	E	V	A
U	O	U	R	O	S	L	U	P	E	R	C
P	G	S	M	H	S	U	O	P	R	I	R
E	E	A	S	J	E	L	E	O	S	N	O
R	A	I	M	D	S	G	W	S	D	T	B
S	E	R	U	M	E	T	A	T	I	B	A
O	A	V	E	I	A	H	H	C	E	I	T
N	I	M	S	H	N	U	E	O	W	S	A
I	E	Y	E	S	S	N	L	B	J	O	M
C	S	A	S	O	O	D	L	E	I	H	S
S	B	I	T	S	N	E	K	P	T	S	O
M	J	O	L	N	I	R	S	L	U	C	S

Page 48

B and F

Page 52

A. Abomination, B. Red Skull, C. Loki

Page 53

There are 14 HYDRA agents

Page 54

"Bring the thunder!"

"Hulk smash!"

"Reporting for duty."

"Iron Man armour: activate!"

Page 57

Pages 60-61

1. Hawkeye 2. Iron Man and Black Widow 3. Avengers Tower 4. Russia 5. Red 6. Gamma 7. Mjolnir 8. Tony Stark 9. Gold 10. S.H.I.E.L.D.